PRINCETON THEOLOGICAL MONOGRAPH SERIES

Dikran Y. Hadidian

General Editor

5

MY FATHER-IN-LAW
MEMORIES OF KARL BARTH

My
Father-In-Law

Memories of Karl Barth

By
Max Zellweger-Barth

Translated by
H. Martin Rumscheidt

PICKWICK PUBLICATIONS
Allison Park, Pennsylvania

Library of Congress Cataloging-in-Publication Data

Zellweger-Barth, Max.
    My father in-law.

      (Princenton theological monograph series ; 5)
      Translation of: Mein Schwiegervater.
      1. Barth, Karl, 1886-1968.   2. Theologians—
Switzerland—Biography.   I. Title.   II. Series.
BX4827.B3Z4513   1986   230'.044'0924   [B]   86-2411
ISBN 0-915138-84-0

Printed and Bound by Publishers Choice Book Manufacturing Co.
Mars, Pennsylvania 16046

Contents

Preface 1

First Encounter 3

Life Together 7

Trip to Copenhagen 19

Trip to Paris 33

Memory Fragments 41

Preface

In the course of the last decade, and even during Karl
Barth's lifetime, there were frequently occasions in small
groups of people when I quite spontaneously related experiences I had had with my father-in-law. I was repeated-
ly asked to put some of them on paper so that Karl Barth
could be better known from that perspective as well.

For a long time I hesitated to do so. I felt it presumptuous to rank myself among the many who had written
"intelligent things," as my father-in-law used to put it,
about Karl Barth and his work.

I also wondered whether such records would not appear
too personal. And yet it is not possible to capture the
"memories" of someone close to you without becoming
personal.

I want to express gratitude to my dear wife for repeated-
ly encouraging me to overcome my reluctance and "simply to start writing in order to see what emerges." That is
why I very much regret the fact that I have not drawn her
much more often into the portraits presented here. I was
constrained to keep strictly to the topic before me. Still,
the cooperation with my spouse in presenting these
memories has brought us together in a special way as we
thought about our father and father-in-law. It is to her,
therefore, that this book is dedicated with deep gratitude.

Max Zellweger-Barth

First Encounter

I came to know Franziska Barth in the summer of 1934. She had come half a year before her parents to Basel in order to study, for she could no longer stand the regimentation that had begun to take quite unimaginable forms at that time in Germany. Since she was enrolled in a piano course with Rudolf Serkin, she spent a week with her grandmother, Mrs. Anna Barth-Sartorius, at Wabern near Berne.

Then, one day, I received a telephone call from Miss Barth asking whether I would mind coming to Wabern in my car and driving her home. Her father was on a brief visit to his mother's and that would be a good opportunity to meet him. I accepted gladly. One day prior to that meeting the new indoor swimming pool near the viaduct in Basel was to be formally opened. This event appeared to me to be a chance to divest my preoccupation facing the visit in Wabern. Yet it did not turn out that way. The pool left me cold; the concentration on Wabern lingered.

That day, September 30, was a day as sunny as a midsummer day. I arrived on time after lunch at the little single family home, located above the city. Miss Barth was waiting for me in the garden. From an open window in the upper floor there sounded the voice of the man whom I came to see "face to face" for the first time even though he was known to me from many of his writings and from newspaper photos. The voice said, "I shall be right down."

After the short, first greeting we sat down in a corner of

the garden— grandmother, father, daughter and I. Karl Barth stuffed his pipe, leaned back in his chair, looked at me and said, "Mr. Zellweger, I would like to ask you something now." This was going to be interesting, I thought, as the future I was hoping for might well depend on whether or not I responded correctly. "What do you think of the position taken by the 'Basler Nachrichten'?" [One of the major daily newspapers of Basel] "Deplorable, Herr Professor," I said (for at that time the stance of the paper towards the Third Reich was not clear. The smile radiating from behind the pipe let me conclude that my answer had hit the nail on the head. Now I could wash down my first fright with some hot coffee. This first question led to a long political discussion which cast the ladies into the position of listeners. Karl Barth was at the very centre of the German church struggle and nearly every new day created for him a different and turbulent situation. His dramatic narration was captivating. A second pot of strong coffee made time fly unnoticed. Only momentarily did I recall that I had not made the trip to Berne to discuss politics or the church struggle.

In the course of the afternoon Karl Barth's sister, Mrs. Gertrud Lindt, a minister's wife, and her four children arrived. They, too, took a close look at me. Eventually I was informed of the family council's decision that Miss Barth and I were to take a drive with those four children to the airport at Belp. The wonderful weather and the car ought not to be wasted! Thus unfolded a new, unexpected turn of events. Small wonder that I was told a few weeks later that

I had not been especially cordial to the children on that occasion. (Twenty two years later, at a family gathering, I referred to this incident and Karl Barth's sister confessed that it had indeed occurred to them at the time that it was not quite in order to let the two of us drive off alone.)

After the prescribed drive on that Sunday afternoon I was anxious to speak with Karl Barth again. I succeeded but failed in relation to one point. He took me to a more or less quiet corner of the large, well-laid dining room table so that we might talk in peace. After noting the existence of distant relationships between us he enquired, with remarkable interest, about my activities in the sales division of the Geigy chemical concern. All my attempts to shape our conversation in a way that would include the person I was most deeply interested in failed utterly.

The day was drawing to an end and the moment of farewell drew closer. Fortunately, before me lay the drive home which we were to take together. As my eleven years older brother, who had also spent the day in Berne, would drive with us, the trip could be undertaken without concern. At one point Karl Barth and his daughter left the living room. I used the occasion to check something quickly in my car, but, alas! as I left I found both standing on the steps leading to the front door, whispering to each other. As I could not retreat I scurried between them without hearing one word.

The tone of our goodbyes gave reason to be hopeful. The drive home provided a uniquely beautiful view of the Alps. At home we parted from my brother, left the car on the square by the cathedral and walked down to the Rhine, very close to the water, and became engaged to be married. After midnight, when I escorted my fiancée back to the parsonage near the cathedral, her residence at that time, the lights were still on in the study of Rev. Eduard Thurneysen. He was the first to learn of our happy event.

Life Together

For Christmas 1936 my father-in-law gave me a chess set. Among the chess pieces was a note which read, "Dear Max! May you stride over the stage of life like a *king*, never be under the thumb of the *queen*, stand always like a *castle*, yet move across fields like a *bishop*, at times climb with me on a horse like a *knight* and, as a result thereof, gain the health of a *pawn* [the German term for that piece is *Bauer*: farmer. trans.], put all that goes against you into *check* and under no circumstances be *check-mated*. This wish for you, your father-in-law."

Throughout his life my father-in-law worked intensely and showed immense productivity, something I have not found to such an extent in anyone else. It is understandable then that being with him was something very special even within the inner circle of the family. That is why I was particularly happy that he regularly telephoned me late on Sunday evenings in order to talk about much that had happened during the week gone by. He did so because of interest and not only because of curiousity which, as he said, was a characteristic of his family.

To this day I still miss his words: "S'isch Sunntig z'obe. . .", it is Sunday evening. At least once a year he would take me out for dinner in the environs of Basel. We told our families that these events were purely 'men's affairs.' Throughout his tenure at the University of Basel I was allowed to be his guest at the annual *dies academicus*. In this way the contact between my father-in-law and me became ever closer. I had lost my own father when I was only two years old. This life together with Karl Barth was, consequently, a great, never expected gift, particularly since I had also found my closest friend in my father-in-law.

During the summer holidays my in-laws and Karl Barth's co-worker, Charlotte von Kirschbaum, often came for a visit. There was always much room in the spacious chalets which we rented. Those visits were the high points for our family.

My father-in-law used to recall with special pleasure two little incidents which took place in 1942 at Grindelwald.

My spouse and I were taking a walk with our four-year-old daughter Ursula through the village when we met a funeral procession outside the cemetery. It was the first time Ursula had seen such a sight and we tried to inform her gently about the procession and the hearse. The child reacted spontaneously, saying, "We must go home quickly to see whether Grandpapa is still alive."

Then one night my father-in-law went up to Ursula's bed in order to say good-night. Just before the little child had asked her mother, after the evening prayer, why people said prayers at all. "It is so that God will hear us when we express our thanks, and guard us against bad things like disease, fire, earthquake or such like." Whereupon Ursula said to her grandfather, "Tomorrow I am not going to pray for once so that finally something frightening will happen, such as an earthquake or a real air alert."

The next year we were again together at Grindelwald.

On October 10, 1943, my father-in-law wrote me among other things that "Fränzeli will have told you in rough outline about my various trips and undertakings (at Gerzensee, Leysin, Safenwil, Geneva, Neuchatel.) This time I have had very satisfying experiences pretty well everywhere, met friendly people and had good audiences. I have really enjoyed our autumnal Switzerland in all its colours and shapes. Something of the joy of being elderly consists in becoming so much more receptive-receptive to nature as well as to the variety of what gladdens us and what is worthy of praise. We, or I, in any case, used to rush by these things when we were younger with impetuous abandon, not noticing how much there is to be thankful for. . . I have to preach for Eduard Thurneysen on October 31 at the Münster, so that he may have a few more days of vacation. I do not like to preach in that church. The environment is not to my taste and I am bothered by Erasmus, who is buried there. But one must not give in to such disinclinations and so nevertheless I am going to do it once again. . ."

In April 1952 my father-in-law asked me to spend ten days with him holidaying in Lugano-Paradiso. I gladly agreed to come even though I was quite concerned whether I could be a satisfactory conversation partner to him for such an extended period. But the mood was so relaxed even during the train trip and so holiday-like—(travelling in the smoking section was, of course, taken for granted)—that my concern proved groundless. During the trip I showed him something I had learned as a child.

When one attaches a key to a long string and the string to the luggage rack, the key will make delightful, contra-rotating pendulum movements in the Gotthard loop-tunnels when the train is in full motion. I had to repeat that experiment in later years.

The holidays moved along in a regulated pattern. After breakfast we took short walks in the countryside; taking a cup of coffee after lunch, the mail of the day was read, usually aloud to one another. Needless to say, it was not a quiet time for resting. At three in the afternoon I had 'free time,' since my father-in-law wanted to work till supper-time in the hotel room. He was preparing his lectures on the doctrine of reconciliation at that time (Church Dogmatics IV/1). "Tea time" would have been abhorrent to him in any case. After supper we would play a game of chess—the average result for the holiday period was 3 to 1 in his favour—or we would go out to some performance. The day ended with a relaxing evening drink.

These nightly intervals, both lighthearted and serious, were propitious hours for me. My father-in-law would lay open his whole life and relate how he had come to enjoy his work so much, the work which in good and bad days, in times of illness, would displace everything else for him right up to the time of his death. It was an enjoyment that he did not "possess" but which was given him anew each day and which bestowed on him the persistence to keep going with that work. He had a modesty and a thankfulness which were constantly apparent. These and his un-shakeable faith in Jesus Christ radiated, unbeknownst to him, a strength that made so much of the half-baked and indifferent things we read and hear insignificant. That is how Karl Barth's declarations became truly worthy of credence and that is also why they shall remain so.

Shortly before that vacation time I had read his book *Protestant Theology in the 19th Century* and was impressed by his masterful description of the personalities of that time. My father-in-law commented, "You know, that is not really as difficult as it may appear at first glance. One simply has to consider first of all what the surrounding world in which people were living looked like, what they wore, what habits their lives had taken on, how they moved and travelled, what they ate, what music was written at their time, etc. Then, after having read the most important writings of the thinkers to be dealt with, one writes on a different piece of paper what positions they took in theology and philosophy and the essential substance for ones presentation will have been gathered." Such a trivialisation of that magnificent work in no way reduced my admiration.

According to the notes I made during the evenings conversation, my father-in-law went on to say that he stood in the place of all those thinkers in as much as their and his actions are wholly under God's judgment. His assessment of each of the personalities described in that book had been guided consistently by the assertion, valid also for them all, "I believe in the forgiveness of sins." "Good heavens, how can we know whether our doings here on earth will eventually be able to stand before God. Perhaps everything I write and say now is all wrong. But I carry on nevertheless, since I feel compelled to do so and since I cannot stop. Beside the judgment which will come upon us all there is also God's grace to which we may deliver ourselves confidently. By that grace we live even today with all our actions. For this reason, and for this reason alone, we may face the future with cheerfulness."

It was unavoidable that some people "tracked down" my father-in-law wherever he spent his holidays. It was difficult to keep people away, particularly on this holiday, when a couple who could claim kinship to Karl Barth wanted to see him. A short meeting at the hotel was agreed upon. It turned out to be a monologue on the part of the couple who alternated in their immense loquaciousness. It was very tiring for the listener. When they discovered that we were planning to go to the theatre that evening, they declared that they would wait for us after the performance. When Papa and I were seated, in high spirits, in our orchestra seats, we spotted the couple high above us in the section of cheap seats. "That affluent people buy such cheap tickets on their holidays must be punished." And that is what happened. We calculated that descending from their height would require considerably more time than it would take us to leave from where we were. Therefore, we departed quickly after the end of the performance, went to a little pub on a side-street and were not discovered. The next day the telephone rang and they told us "how easily people can lose one another in the crowd after a play."

After meals my father-in-law preferred to stay inside the hotel, since one could not really concentrate on significant things in the garden, not even while reading the mail. (I have seen him work only rarely on the large patio outside his study in Basel.) One bright day I did succeed in persuading him to make an exception and spend time outside. But, to my horror, I noticed that on every one of the chaise-lounges, at head-level, there were round imprints of the previous guests' hair pomade. Papa sat down without a word, full of scepticism. When he arose, he declared that he would never again seat himself on one of these grease-bowls. They were meant for better folk and not for him. He had thought from the beginning that things would not turn out well. Sunshine or not, sitting outside after a meal was once and for all a thing of the past. The yellow, musty leather armchairs, filled with the scent of stale smoke, were back in favour. In addition to the letters read aloud my father-in-law would hand me bundles of older letters and articles of every description, saying that we would discuss them later in the evening. All I could do was protest that I was not a "superperson" like he and would require a whole week to digest what he could do in only a few hours.

On Good Friday we attended divine services in the diaspora congregation of Lugano and took communion. As we left the church we noticed that a dog show was just about to open across the street. My father-in-law said, "Let's go there right away, for that is a good opportunity."

I hesitated a moment and asked whether we should do that immediately after having received communion. He replied that that was no problem for him. Dogs are creatures of God, like us. Why should we not go and look at them and rejoice in them?

As we talked about this matter that evening, the following became clear to me: the celebration of communion in the church or in small circles is the confirmation of the sacrifice Christ made for us on the cross, a confirmation he ordained and which we are to make ever anew. That *happening* on the cross has validity once and for all and accompanies us in the good and in the bad times of our lives. It cannot be disengaged, therefore, from our daily existence. Because that is so, we are set free from the religious constrictions which we believe we have to lay upon ourselves after the celebration of communion. —My father-in-law expressed his regret that communion was not a regular occurrence in Protestant worship. In this matter Roman Catholics are clearly ahead of Protestants.

At the dog show there was a magnificent Appenzeller sheepdog, which my father-in-law liked so much that he seriously considered taking him home to Basel. He thought the dog could become a footrest under his desk and would cause similar joy to the other members of the household. It took me no little effort to dissuade my father-in-law; he had already settled on a price and was enquiring about the diet. Two arguments persuaded him: for the dog being a footrest would only be a "dog's life" and for him personally it would mean walking the dog twice a day. (I knew how reluctantly he interrupted his work for reasons of health by such "walks".) The plan was dropped.

With regard to work: One Sunday afternoon in Basel I found Karl Barth leaning over his desk working on his Dogmatics. I could not help admonishing him to give himself a little more rest, at least on Sundays. We read, after all, in the Bible that on one day of the week we are to let our work come to a halt. He responded by saying that nowhere did it say in the Bible that we were not to read or occupy ourselves with that on Sundays. In his work he was about nothing other than what the Bible was itself about. He had no reason at all to have a bad conscience about what he was doing and would therefore continue working as he did.

Whenever my father-in-law set out early in the day during his vacations on a solo walk, he always overestimated his strength and returned to a delayed lunch completely exhausted and without appetite. Once he tackled the San Salvatore mountain and another time (during another holiday trip), from Locarno, the Madonna des Sasso. He lost the trail and, as he told later, "nearly plummeted down the mountain as he crisscrossed ravine and rock." Those who know the region can well picture such precarious wanderings. He unfortunately sustained injuries to his hands and feet and had to rearrange the program of the day. A boat trip from Lugano-Paradiso to Gandria and back proceeded without problems. Against my protests he insisted on rowing without my assistance. I was told to enjoy the country and lakeside, which I did, while continuously enjoining him to slow down the pace.

The end of the holiday was upon us. At the railroad station the couple referred to earlier were awaiting us on the platform to say good-bye, "since we missed one another the other day." "By the way," the husband continued, "I noticed just now that the first four coaches of your train are third class compartments. (In those days trains still had such a class.) You may just as well move up the platform now." My father-in-law responded dryly, "When I go on holiday with my son-in-law we travel second-class. I wish you still happy holidays." In Arth-Goldau we parted company. My father-in-law went on to Zürich. I still see him standing on the platform waving his handkerchief and hear him calling out, "We'll do that again."

I could not have surmised at that moment that in the years between 1954 and 1962 seven more such holiday times would follow. They were all equally joyous for me. The days at Brione above Minusio, where we went five times, hold special memories for me since on occasion very interesting friends of my father-in-law came to visit, such as Prof. Hermann Diem, Prof. Helmut Gollwitzer, Dr. Gustav Heinemann, Prof. Ernst Wolf and others. The topic of these conversations, in which I was a silent participant, was often the internal politics of Germany. Other relatives and friends present were not excluded from those talks.

For a time it seemed, on account of mutual misunderstanding, that the holidays in 1960 would not be taken together. My father-in-law wrote me concerning that, among other things, on March 5. "You see, whenever you, in appearance or in actual fact, detect a twitch at the corners of my mouth, you must never think I "mean" or could "mean" or have "meant" this or that and that that is serious and needs to be rectified and the like. Look, I indeed teach and write "dogmatics," (as long as God has patience with me) but I am basically not a dogmatic person. I go from one day to the next and always try to learn something new so that no one needs to fear my "meanings," least of all you. I do not want to compare myself to Blumhardt, but I have always liked, among much else, that in response to someone who said to him, 'but Reverend Blumhardt, you said one day. . .,' he is said to have replied, 'What did I say? I said nothing at all.' You have to take me somewhat like that, too. We will sit together in some hotel armchairs some other time, won't we? Obviously things did not succeed this year because neither of us knew at first what it was we wanted and then "supposed" right past each other. And things will turn out all right as long as it will not be too cold for you where you are but, rather, cozy in every respect. (My spouse and I had planned to go to Schönried in the Canton of Berne.)

"Wonderful! Fränzeli just called. You are still there and what is more, we are to be with you in half an hour! So, why this letter? You should get it despite all. Therefore, affectionately and in joy, your Papa."

A few days later we did travel to Brione after all -The joyful essence of those joint vacations was the suggestion of my father-in-law to compose a pamphlet together with the title: "How to Spend One's Holidays Sensibly."

Trip to Copenhagen

On February 23, 1963, the newspapers reported that Prof. Dr. Karl Barth was to receive the Danish Sonning Prize, an award granted in recognition of outstanding merit on behalf of European culture. Among earlier recipients were Winston Churchill, Albert Schweitzer, Igor Stravinsky, Niels Bohr and Bertrand Russell. My father-in-law asked me by telephone whether I felt like accompanying him to Copenhagen and to the ceremony on April 19, when the prize would be given to him. If I wished to come, he would add to the acknowledgment of the invitation that my presence was indispensable to him for the trip. Then I would surely receive an invitation. I accepted without hesitation. Nothing was dearer or more valuable to me, next to my family, than frequent times together with my father-in-law. A formal invitation came back promptly. I took from it, perhaps mistakenly, that my hosts regarded me rather as an irksome appendage.

On a beautifully sunny day, April 18, my spouse drove us to the airport at Kloten, for the shuttle service from the airport at Basel was still quite unsatisfactory at that time. When a clerk of Swissair enquired whether we wanted to increase the regular amount of accident insurance, I asked my father-in-law about it and he said, "Yes, that is good for the grieving survivors." My spouse stood some distance away and learned about that comment only after our return. The higher the Caravelle aircraft climbed the more holiday like we felt. My father-in-law ordered whiskey, whereas I preferred a Vermouth so that I would not arrive in Copenhagen after the relatively short flight in too shaky a condition. Later on I did not mind when my father-in-law reported that while he drank his whiskey I was enjoying my herbal tea! We both agreed that the Danish flight attendants radiated a very special charm. That relatively uneventful flight to Copenhagen remains unforgettable. The runway ends directly at the shoreline so that, at low-level flight, one believes until the final moment that the landing gear will scrape the huge and mighty icefloes that are still there in April and look so threatening.

The Rector of the University of Copenhagen, Prof. Dr. rer. pol. Carl Iversen and his spouse welcomed us most cordially at the airport and accompanied us to the Hotel d'Angleterre. It is located very near the Royal Palace and looks like a smaller version of Blair House in Washington, opposite the White House, the residence of the President's official guests. The most beautiful apartment, usually reserved for royal visitors, was assigned to my father-in-law. When we were alone, admiring the magnificent appointments of the sitting room, the reception chamber and the other rooms, my delight was very great. My father-in-law observed, "Indeed, quite appropriate to the present occasion." Already the telephone was ringing in the adjoining study. The time for me to assume my assigned duties had come. The schedule for interviews had to be established; an untold number of letters and telegrams had arrived and needed to be opened; flowers had to be received. My own room was located next to Papa's and left nothing to be desired in regard to elegance. As there were no more theatre tickets available for that first evening we amused ourselves with Charlie Chaplin's film *Modern Times*.

The following, most important day, began with a walk which focussed primarily on the landmark of Copenhagen, the famous Mermaid. In the afternoon the solemn awarding of the Sonning Prize took place. The Rector of the University himself presented it to my father-in-law. Prior to this the invited guests had assembled and after some refreshment lined up, two by two, for the procession to the Festival Hall. At the head were the Rector and Karl Barth, followed by Mrs. Sonning and me, arm in arm. As we processed leisurely and I hummed to myself "Das gibt's nur einmal, das kommt nicht wieder" (This happens only once and never comes again) there sounded marvelous music in the distance, without doubt Mozart. At that same moment my father-in-law turned, radiant on account of Mozart, delighting in the couple that processed behind him. The hall was more than filled. All present rose respectfully from their seats and remained standing until the guests had taken the seats reserved for them. How pleasing were the first two movements of Mozart's String Quartet in D-major, K.V.275! Thereafter Prof. Dr. theol. Niels Hansen Soe brought greetings, followed by the presentation of the Sonning Prize and the reading of the *laudatio* by the Rector of the University. He then invited the illustrious guest to deliver his announced speech. Besides expressing thanks for the honor bestowed upon him, Karl Barth spoke about his relation to Søren

Page 22

Kierkegaard. Since his comments about this great Danish theologian were not exclusively complimentary, they were received with mixed feelings.

What Karl Barth said, in brief form, was this.[1] While the young Barth often made positive reference to Kierkegaard, he would later register particular reservations about Kierkegaard's negations, his individualism in relation to human salvation and his anthropocentrism. In Kierkegaard there are to be found rudiments of the existential philosophy of Heidegger, Jaspers and Sartre. And yet he, Karl Barth, remains faithful to this day to Kierkegaard's "reveille."

> In light of these later insights, I am and remain thankful as before to Kierkegaard for the immunization he gave me in those days. I am and remain filled with deep respect for the genuinely tragic nature of his life and for the extraordinary intellectual luster of his work. I consider him a teacher into whose school every theologian must go once. Woe to the one who has missed it! So long as one does not remain in or return to it! His teaching is, as he himself once said, "a pinch of spice" for the food, not the food itself, which is the task of right theology to offer to the church and thus to all humans. The Gospel is first the *glad* news of God's YES to human beings. It is

1. For the full text of the address see Karl Barth, *Fragments Grave and Gay*, ed. by H. Martin Rumscheidt, London: Wm. Collins and Sons, 1971, or *Canadian Journal of Theology*, Vol. XI, No.1, 1965, pp. 3-7.

secondly the news which the *congregation* must pass on to the whole world. It is thirdly the news from on *high*. These are three aspects, in relation to which I had to do further study, after my meeting Kierkegaard, in the school of other teachers.

The festive occasion came to a dignified conclusion in the playing of the final two movements of the Mozart Quartet.

There was not much time left between the celebration and the gala dinner given in honour of the recipient at the Hotel d'Angleterre. There was just enough time to speak with two waiting newspaper reporters. We went to our rooms to change our attire. My father-in-law remarked briefly that he would telephone me if something were not quite in order with his clothes. That warning caused me to shave at top speed, and to put on the not altogether daily attire with blinding haste. And lo! the telephone rang. "Max, a number of things are not as they should be with my attire. Could you come over quickly?" A nice mess! For some strange reason I had had a premonition in Basel that something might happen in this matter. Therefore, I had packed certain spare parts in my case, such as a white bow tie, several studs and the like. I rushed to his room. My father-in-law sat on a chair and showed me how the shirt front popped out of the vest every time he stood up. On closer inspection I discovered to my dismay that it was no dress shirt at all, but in fact merely a starch-stiffened shirt front that had to be tied with ribbons over an ordinary shirt. This monster had been recommended in the store where he had rented the tails, his own having become too tight for him. I noticed that one of the ribbons had already come off. It was a feat to accomplish the necessary fastening with the one remaining ribbon while not causing the wearer too much constriction. Then there was the tie! It was black, instead of white. Triumphantly I produced a white one from my pocket, not pre-tied at that. (People, especially in the United States, regard it as most uncouth when someone wears a factory-tied bow tie.) After dogged attempts to bring the collar into position with a fitting stud the placing of the bow tie began. What's the matter, I thought. I had had no trouble putting mine on while now all that emerged was a knob. Finally I concluded that it is one thing to put a tie on oneself but quite another to put it on someone else. I recalled that as a young man in New York I had asked the proprietor of a tiny haberdashery on a sidestreet off Wall Street to show me how to make a beautiful bow with such a tie. He climbed on a chair since he was of a small stature, embraced me from behind (replete with the smell of garlic) and placed the bow tie as if on himself. That is exactly what I did then with my father-in-law, without the use of a chair. At that moment the apartment bell rang. I heard nothing, or rather, I did not want to hear anything. A minute later it rang again. The third ring was reinforced by loud knocks. Papa said, "It seems that we are having company. Would you check, please. We have enough rooms to receive them." Knowing what was going on I rushed to the door.

Two attendants in red livery had come. One of them said that the ladies and gentlemen downstairs were ready. I looked at my watch. We were already fifteen minutes late. I passed on the message. Papa reacted utterly calmly. "Max, it really pleases me to see you for once really perturbed. I have not seen that till this day. And the little drops on your forehead that look like small pearls become you not at all badly." What was I to say? I could not get angry. I liked my father-in-law far too much. The best was to remain silent for the time being and to concentrate wholly on getting that bow tie in place. And lo! I succeeded on the first try. Only the reserve studs had to be forced with brute force through the much too narrow eyes of the stiffened "monster," and soon my father-in-law stood in full splendour in front of the mirror. One last thing needed attention: my "pearls" had to be removed. While doing that I noticed that my collar and my own, once so stiff shirt front manifested signs of dissolving.

As if nothing had happened we descended the stairs with heads held high. The guests were waiting in several salons and we had difficulty finding the Rector. He set out right away to introduce everyone present, by now already lined up, to my father-in-law unless they had already met him during the celebration at the University. It was touching how concerned my father-in-law was to make sure that I, too, was a part of the introduction ceremonies. The great doors to the state room opened. There were about one hundred guests. As a secretary called out their names, they were shown their seats by attendants around a single table which, on account of its length and width could hardly be taken in at one glance. Looking at the dinner guests, all those ladies and gentlemen dressed, as it were, for a royal banquet, the gleaming jewels and the countless medals, the table decorated in the middle with a veritable rose garden, I felt as if I were in a fairy tale. My father-in-law sat at the centre of the table, flanked by the Minister of Ecclesial Affairs, Mr. Bodil Koch and Mrs. Sonning. I had been assigned a seat diagonally across from him which suited me just fine since I could observe whether Karl Barth's attire remained in proper order. Everything stayed in its assigned place. Only the bow tie had a slight list to the right which no one other than I noticed.

The Rector delivered the obligatory welcome speech in which he referred anew to the great significance of his guest of honour and of his work. What he had read of that work remains an open question. A little later he announced that Karl Barth would speak. It turned out to be a short address since, as he put it, he had already spoken long enough in the afternoon. He found words of thanks for the attention shown him, full of meaning, and concluded his speech by remarking that "my son-in-law will now supplement my comments." The Rector sank back in his chair disconcerted. I received a stinging glance that was clearly not meant for me personally but that went through me into some remote distance. It seemed to say, "What else is the recipient this year going to dish up! First he lets this illustrious company wait for a half hour and now I have to give the floor over to an insignificant companion of his. All of that is quite contrary to protocol." But what else could he do but knock against his glass and declare, "Ladies and Gentlemen, it is my privilege to call now also upon Mr. . . ." Alerted from earlier such occasions, at which my father-in-law had called on me to speak even though I was not prepared for it, I had lodged three key words in my mind just in case, although I was certain that it would not arise during these ceremonies. The words were: thanks, Denmark and Switzerland, two small countries with very different forms of government and their commonality within the European Free Trade Area. They were sufficient to rescue me from major embarrassment. After the dinner my father-in-law observed, "Good! The reason why the Swiss Ambassador did not speak is because you anticipated the only topic which would have suited him."

The remainder of the evening took the usual form for occasions of this importance. My father-in-law was set upon from all sides and overloaded with questions. Even after midnight, when the Rector declared the event to be formally at an end, individual conversations during the goodbyes ended unwillingly, since the rare opportunity for personal contact with Karl Barth had, for good reasons, to be grasped. In spite of the great strain on him my father-in-law fell asleep right away, whereas I had some difficulty in coming to terms with consciousness, half dreaming and half sleep.

The next morning a minister couple met us to take us on

a sightseeing tour of the city. After viewing Frederiksborg Castle from the outside and the inside my father-in-law grew tired. I agreed immediately with him when he whispered to me as we came in sight of Christiansborg Castle that we could do without a guided tour of this castle. The sight-seeing tour came to an end earlier than planned. Even so, other people were waiting remorselessly in the hotel lobby. This time it was the journalists.

A question period had been scheduled for the afternoon in the assembly hall of the University. The attentiveness and enthusiasm of the audience, almost exclusively Danish students, were impressive and it took a long time before the lively discussion could be brought to a close.

The amiable dean of the faculty of theology, Prof. Dr. N. H. Soe and his spouse were not to be denied the privilege of inviting the honored guest to their splendid villa for supper. Their colleagues in the university and many other friends were also invited. There is a pleasant custom in Denmark. At table the host speaks twice, first to welcome the guests and, after a certain time, about other things. This adds much to the merriment of the table company. My father-in-law spiced his speech, as was his custom, with humor and I followed him, without any signal, with my "supplement." After dinner the conversation focussed on theology in the form of questions to Karl Barth. He looked tired so that no one was surprised that we said good night earlier than desired shortly before midnight. I was, therefore, all the more delighted when my father-in-law took my hand in the taxi and said, "Now begins the relaxed part of the evening. We have to let all that has happened this day pass before us in review." No sooner had we sat down in a corner of the lounge in our hotel than, much to our surprise, Mrs. Sonning walked toward us. She sat down at our table and we did not lack subjects to talk about. We began to talk without any preliminaries about the meaning of life. The widow of the donor of the prize declared categorically that she kept to the fundamental axiom 'do what is right and fear no one' and that she had fared well by it throughout her life. My father-in-law replied in his genial way that according to his own insight and experience this axiom, while valuable in itself, does not entirely suffice to permit people to live their lives according to the purpose given to all existence. One would at least have to consider that human activity is not to be understood out of itself but as the activity of the creature God created. In such dependence on and to God our activity does not become and end in itself. In the service of others, then, our lives take on meaning. Indeed we cannot decide ourselves whether what we do, even from the best of motives, is "right."

In his *Church Dogmatics* III/4, p. 327-9, Karl Barth says this:

> The creaturely existence of humankind is as such not its property; it is a loan. As such it must be held in trust. It is not, therefore, under the control of people. But in the broadest sense it is meant for the service of God. 'Know that our God indeed is

Lord, and for His glory hath us made, t'is wholly on this gracious Word, the life of everyone is stayed.' This is the simplest information that can be given concerning the fact and meaning of life. Nor is it the result of self-reflection on the part of us humans. It depends entirely on the fact that God addresses us. It derives from the Word of God as the Word of our Creator and Lord. And implicitly it is the information which is given concerning all other life and the reality and the meaning of life in general.

The questions that journalists put to my father-in-law during those days left nothing to be desired in terms of superficiality. Of greatest interest was the use of the money which was part of the Sonning Prize, amounting to about 60,000 Swiss Francs. (One third of it was promised to me that very night for use by the Protestant City mission of Basel, of which I was the president at the time; another third went to the Basel Mission Society, whose mission work was overseas; part of the remaining third went to the poor-box of the parish of Mülligen, a village in the Canton of Aargau from which the Barth family had originally come.) The ever-recurring question was, "What are you going to do with the money?" "I shall most likely buy a white elephant or a Rolls Royce." The journalists went home satisfied. Next day the large-print headline of a tabloid read: "Professor Barth: a White Elephant." In this way one episode after another passed by us in our conversations. Very disturbing, however, was something else to be read in the papers! One reported, word for word, the following: "What is noteworthy about the Sonning Prize is that the money is derived from the profit made from houses that are in scandalous condition and for whom poor people have to pay fearfully high rent." Karl Barth said about that, "Had I known about these circumstances before I accepted the prize, I do not know whether. . . ."

By then that was all in the past, and we came to this conclusion: poor people contribute with their money but without any knowledge to the awarding of a prize honoring special merit on behalf of European culture. The recipient accepts the money in full innocence but does not keep it for himself. Instead he divides it among institutions whose work is to share goods with the poor. It seemed to balance the equation somehow. Our high spirits were kept high by this solution and we reflected upon further tales about the uncontrollable circulation of money.

At two o'clock in the morning the lounge closed its doors. We returned to our apartment and talked for another hour, this time about our so questionable behaviour here on earth. My father-in-law believed firmly that eventually we would have to give an account for every vain word our lips utter. It was a serious matter and occupied me much that night. My last concern that evening was that I would arouse my father-in-law in time since our flight home was departing very early. So it was that on a Sunday morning we left the still sleeping Copenhagen and were welcomed home at Kloten by our 'non-mourning survivors?'

Trip to Paris

In August, 1963, my father-in-law informed me that another trip was "in the wind." Would I be interested in accompanying him again. It was so pleasant in Copenhagen, he said. But this time he had to go to Paris. At the beginning of November he was to receive an honorary doctorate from the Sorbonne. I spontaneously expressed my great joy that he would again think of me to accompany him. How could I have hesitated even one moment with my yes? Still, I added, there were certain aspects of the trip to Copenhagen that stuck in my memory which might better not be repeated in Paris. I would, as it were, make it a condition of my going that in external matters, including those of preparing for the trip, he would, as I literally said to him, "obey my every word." He concurred without reserve. Thereupon we agreed that my father-in-law would look after the intellectual matters and I the technical aspects and that each would assume full responsibility for his own area of concern. Subsequently this agreement completely proved its worth.

My father-in-law responded to the invitation of "Monsieur le Recteur Jean Roche, Presidént du Conseil de l'Université de Paris" with the same statement he had made to Copenhagen, namely, that he could undertake the journey only in the company of his son-in-law. I received a cordial invitation forthwith. The day of travel itself, Wednesday, November 6, was quite burdensome. When we arrived at the Grand Hôtel du Louvre we were told that the elevators were out of order due to a power shortage, the duration of which was unknown. We would, therefore, have to use the staircase to reach our rooms on the fourth floor. Since the hotel was completely filled, a change of rooms was out of the question. We had no alternative, in view of my father-in-law's heart condition, but to climb each step with extreme care and to take a long rest on each floor. Fortunately this unpleasant beginning had no ill after-effects.

It was not possible to take a rest after lunch, which had been brought to our rooms, since the ceremony reopening the Faculty of Protestant Theology at the University of Paris began at 2:30 pm. The dean and the council of professors of that faculty had invited us to attend the ceremony because Dr. W. A. Visser t'Hooft was to be awarded the honorary doctorate at that time. When during his words of welcome the dean announced the presence of Karl Barth, the closely packed crowd in the festively decorated hall welcomed that fact with enthusiastic applause. The opening address was delivered by Reverend M. Carrez. His topic was "Confidence in the Self According to the Apostle Paul." The time following the ceremony was filled with questions and answers. Many old clergy, friends and students stood in line for their turn for a short handshake or brief talk. I observed the goings on from a distance where many people came over, introduced themselves and told me how, when and where they had met Karl Barth before. Here, too, there was impressive respect for Karl Barth, specifically from the Protestant congregation of Pasteur M. Boegner. That evening we went to a supper to which the Reformed Church of France had invited us. We returned to our hotel at a late hour and, after a brief night cap, we went to our rooms.

The "séance solemnelle de rentrée de l'Université de Paris, en présence de Monsieur le Ministre de l'éducation nationale" was to take place at 10:00 a.m the next day in the Great Amphitheatre of the Sorbonne. My father-in-law was in fine spirits at breakfast. I had ordered a taxi for 9:00 a.m which he thought was much too early. We could spend the time much better if we talked another half hour over coffee. When I reminded him of the responsibilities I had accepted for our stay in Paris, he agreed right away. As it turned out, as soon as we had left the hotel at 9:00 o'clock we ran into a traffic jam in one of those side streets which Parisian taxi drivers like to drive on. We were there for half an hour. It was 9:45 a.m when we arrived at the Sorbonne. Unfortunately (!) that was just the time of the changing of the Garde Républicaine positioned in front of the Sorbonne. My father-in-law held me back by my arm, pointed excitedly to the old uniforms and remarked that we now had the opportunity to compare this change of guards with that of the Swiss Army. We reluctantly decided that we did not have time to watch when I said, with a sigh, that we had not come to Paris for this, and that time was pressing. After much searching we found the door to the rector's chamber where the ten candidates for honorary doctorates were to robe. We came upon a scramble of people waiting for the order of the procession into the festive hall. There was no time, much to our regret, to look at all the medals, exhibited in magnificent cases, which were to be presented to the new doctors. But what of it? My father-in-law *was* present and I reached my reserved seat at the front in good time.

To the strains of the Marseillaise the procession entered the wide-domed building. Above the platform, under the large painting by Puvis de Chavannes, hung groupings of the flags of the countries represented by those to be honored with these doctorates, including the Swiss flag. Among the guests were the Swiss ambassador Soldati, members of the diplomatic corps, the Papal Nuncio, as well as representatives of the Reformed Church of France among whom, of course, was Pastor Marc Boegner.

Through the awarding of this honorary doctorate Karl Barth received a unique honor, for it was an unusual citation. Never before had a Protestant theologian been awarded an honorary doctorate by the Sorbonne.

By virtue of the separation of church and state the Sorbonne has no faculty of theology. Therefore, the citation for Karl Barth was read by the Dean of the Faculté des Lettres et Science Humaine. He referred specifically to the literary activity of the theologian from Basel and to the integrity of the position he took in the thirties as an academic in regard to the violent actions of Hitler's state. When Barth stepped forward to have the *épitoge*, symbol of this special degree, pinned on his Basel University academic gown, an applause broke forth which was unlike any the other recipients had been accorded. One of the reporters present concluded from this that "it became apparent from this demonstration how highly Karl Barth is regarded as a human being and what significance is attributed to his life's work."

The dean of the faculty which had unanimously proposed the name of Karl Barth for an honorary doctorate, Prof. André Aymard, gave an extensive laudatory speech. Here are some of his remarks. "The philosophers nominate a theologian, even though he does not want to be a philosopher. In earlier centuries the Sorbonne excommunicated and banned Protestant theologians. Today the University honors one of them. It does so on account of the great qualities which this theologian possesses as a thinker and author of a comprehensive scholarly work. Even though Barth teaches that people are justified by God's grace alone, he is no gloomy prophet. At the centre of his teaching stands God's coming down to humankind and the dignity of each human being as a consequence. Often older people become narrow and hardened. The old Barth, however, manifests largesse and magnanimity that reminds one of Goethe. He demonstrates great openness toward cultural values. We are indebted to him for his important studies of Mozart, Rousseau and Hegel. But he also addressed problems of the contemporary world. The Roman Catholic church, too, is touched by the strength of his thought and the flexibility of his sense for what is human. Diverse controversies have arisen over Barth. But in a time when all people of good will seek after concord, the work of this theologian from Basel is one of the sources from which we may draw new inspiration." As was to be expected, there was to be no end of handshaking after this ceremony as well. Finally my father-in-law was able to get away from the crowd and we exchanged impressions over a peaceful meal.

We met at 5:00 p.m in the hotel lobby shortly before we were to get dressed for the gala dinner at the Sorbonne. A waiter recommended that we try a specialty of the house, a drink called "Vodka double mixed special Grand Hôtel." My father-in-law acceded right away. I did the same, so as not to deny something to Papa and to avoid a situation like that of my "herbal tea" on the flight to Copenhagen. The enjoyment of the treat we were served nearly endangered my sense of responsibility, but the concentration needed to change attire and tie bow ties remained intact. (In Basel my father-in-law reported that I would have liked a second vodka but that time had run out for that.)

The dinner on the upper floor of the Sorbonne was a splendid occasion. The guests were seated at one long and five smaller tables. It was the express wish of all present that in view of the large number of honorary doctorands there should be no speeches. I had been seated next to a member of the interior ministry. My neighbour was very eloquent and openminded so that time flew by too quickly. Later my father-in-law spoke almost exclusively to the Papal Nuncio, Msgr. Marella, with considerable agreement it seemed. The gathering broke up early so that we had time for an hour of conversation at the hotel.

A television interview was scheduled for the following day to which my father-in-law looked forward with his customary calmness. Karl Barth's interviewer was the theology professor Georges Casalis from Paris. Pleased that the sojourn in this beautiful city ended to everyone's satisfaction, we returned home by train on the evening of the same day, cheerful as always.

Memory Fragments

On one occasion my father-in-law and I spent the night in a hotel in Geneva. I asked him in the morning how he had slept. "Badly." "Why?" "Instead of a pillow I had a long thick sausage that I had to force under my head but which was much too high for me to get any sleep on. And there were no blankets either. All I had was a large cube to place on my body. It was not until morning that I discovered that the blanket was hidden in the sausage and the pillow in the cube-like package. By that time it was too late."

We went to have breakfast. As we were taking our first sip of coffee there came the sounds of a Mozart quartet from a radio nearby. Sausage and cube were forgotten and we listened silently to the glorious strains of which Papa knew every single bar. I asked him afterwards whether he ever wanted to hear any other music than that of Mozart. He replied that for him it was thus: during the playing of compositions by other composers he always thinks how beautiful it would be if he could listen at that moment to Mozart's music for then time would not be wasted. After the quartet had ended the question arose almost by compulsion as to whether it had been sheer coincidence that at that very time of day, at the right moment, there had been a transmission not of pop music but of Mozart. It led to a long conversation about predestination and coincidence in the course of which my father-in-law expressed his view on the matter. It is another example of how quickly a carefree, yes even rollicking conversation can end in very serious comments. "We won't probe any further why we heard Mozart today. Instead, we will simply take that fact as a gift to this day."

On my thirty fifth birthday my father-in-law sent congratulations and made the following, astonishing comment: "So, Max, from now on things are only going downhill for you. Today you crossed over the high point of your life." It took me months to find out what lay behind that statement, but I finally succeeded. At the age of 35 my father-in-law had written his commentary on Romans at Safenwil. He confessed to me that he regarded the completion of that work as the high point of his life. Why should the course of my life not be analogous to his?!

When Karl Barth moved to a house in the Bruderholz, a part of Basel located above the downtown area, he had to take the streetcar to get to his lectures and seminars at the university. He used to look at the advertisements displayed in the streetcars. As a result he once brushed up his own poetic talents. On March 2, 1956, he sent me the following "suggestions for advertising specialists, prepared while travelling routes 15 and 16 of the Basel Transit Commission. It has become my lot now to ride the streetcar much more often but, as you can see, I do so not without profit or in a state of mental inactivity." Here is a sample:

Such ohne anderswo zu pröbeln
Behaglichkeit in *Schweizermöbeln!*

(Don't look for comfort far and wide; instead
sleep in a Swiss-made feather-bed.)

Lauf, kauf und lies in grösster Schnelle
die schöne Zeitschrift *Annabelle!*

(Run, buy and read in greatest haste
Annabelle, the magazine of those with taste.)

Als bessern Herrn mich jeder kennt
Ich putz mich nur mit *Pepsodent.*

('A better man' - so says each friend,
since I use only Pepsodent.)

Kennst Du's noch nicht, Du armer Wicht:
Luxram, das einzig wahre Licht?

(You have not heard? You suffer blight.
Luxram's the only bulb to give true light.)

Nein! länger lass ich mich nicht lumpen:
Ich rauche nur noch *Rössli-Stumpen.*

(No one again will say: that armadillo!
Mine from now will be the Rössli-cigarillo.)

Ich esse *Samosan* am Morgen
Und bin dann weiter ohne Sorgen.

(I enjoy Samosan for the morrow
and move about quite without sorrow.)

Ich esse *Samosan* am abend
Mich für die ganze Nacht erlabend.

(I enjoy Samosan as well at night
for then my sleep turns out truly right.)

Ich esse *dauernd* Samosan
Sieht man mirs nicht von Weitem an?

(In fact I eat it night and day.
It shows from even far away.)

Geh, hol - so spricht zum Kind die Mutter
Bei *Althaus-Wyss* die Tafel - Butter.

(Go to Althaus-Wyss, I heard Mum utter,
and bring us home a pound of butter.)

Wie Buchman in der Oxford Gruppe,
Herrscht *Knorr* in jeder guten Suppe.

(What Buchman was to the Oxford Group
that Knorr is surely for all good soup.)

Holz, Kohlen, Heizöl - hei juchheh!
Bringt dir ins Haus die *Heilsarmee*.

(Wood, coal and fuel - ah! what glee!
brings you your Salvation Army.)

Es kaufte schon der Dichter Rilke
Rasierzeug nur bei Firma *Wilke*.

(His shaving needs the poet Rilke
bought only in the house of Wilke.)

Der Mann mit so gesunder Miene
Isst sicher *Lora*-Margarine.

(A man of such a spendid mien
surely eats Lora-Margarine.)

Hol Hosen dir, du armer Zwerg,
Bei *Salathé* am Spalenberg.

(Salathé in the Spalengerg we recommend
for the pants that surely make the gent.)

Empfohlen sei dem Herrn, der Dame
K. B. als Fachmann für Reklame.

(Dear Sir and Madame, not to be missed
is K. B., your advertising specialist.)[2]

When our son Dieter attended high school he went once
a week for lunch to the Bruderholz. On those occasions his

grandfather would have long conversations with him alone. When other guests were present, even if they were renowned people like Hans Küng, they were told before the meal that even for that day the practice would not be changed. The conversations with Dieter followed an established procedure. Events in the city and school were discussed, then the music lessons and his leisure time. News from home was introduced by describing the atmosphere there in the form of a weather synopsis, using terms from "sunny" to "heavy overcast." For example, the question: "Are there any signs of a thunderstorm around the family table and, if so, why?"

Telling jokes was an important component of these conversations. The boy had to tell at least two each time. If he failed to do so, there was no second helping of sausage. There were three categories of jokes: those which could be told in polite company, those to be told in the inner circle of the family only and those to be told strictly to grandpapa alone.

Those conversations at times created a good deal of commotion for our family. Often Dieter came by the house after class on his bicycle, explaining that he knew *one* joke only. After a few weeks I had run dry myself. At times my father-in-law would ask me whether Dieter had heard such and such a joke that he could really not understand on his own from me or at school. We parents grew

---

2. The "translation" of Barth's rhymes are by the translator. They claim no precise accuracy in rendering the originals but only some of their flavor.

more circumspect at that time in our own conversations since everything eventually reached the Bruderholz in an expanded version.

Fortunately I quickly discovered and cancelled a further condition which had been added to those conversations without my knowledge. It was called "things concerning which your father stated: you need not necessarily tell this to your grandfather."

Towards the end of that period Karl Barth's book *Evangelical Theology - an Introduction* appeared. The author had decided to familiarize his grandson with its content. This way chapter by chapter was discussed in many private sessions in which the grandfather proceeded with exactitude yet with gentle attentiveness to the youthful age of his pupil, answering all questions in a similar manner. What a privilege to find ones pleasure in theology through ones grandfather!

One of the best known characteristics of Karl Barth was the fearlessness with which he expressed openly what he thought about church, politics or personal life, whether it was by word of mouth or in writing. He paid little heed to how it would effect those to whom it was addressed. There are two incidents particularly which I recall. A well-known person had delivered a speech in the assembly hall of the University of Basel, followed by discussion. Afterwards we sat together with the speaker, drinking beer. After a while my father-in-law said to him, "Would you explain something to me. You delivered a truly splendid speech. How, then, is it possible that you failed so utterly in the subsequent discussion?"

In the course of a military festivity a high-ranking officer addressed his subordinates. After that he sat down at a table with Karl Barth in order to get to know him. Soon, however, he had to hear words that he had not expected. My father-in-law told him that his speech had not been bad as such, but that it was, to all intents and purposes, a common, garden-variety speech. It could have been delivered just as well in Japan. But on an occasion like the one at hand, it would have been proper to have said something specifically Swiss, of significance only for the Swiss army.

I know that Karl Barth told many ministers quite clearly, be it by admonition or praise, what he thought about their sermons without respect for the person. After an Easter day service of worship he had attended he told me that the sermon had begun with the words: "The day of Easter—the day of joy." "That is exactly how it must *not* go," he added. The end of the sermon must not be at the beginning. Instead, the sermon has to be constructed in such a way that the listeners discern what Easter is about, so that their joy grows bigger and bigger and they are enabled to join in the conviction established by the sermon that issues in the exclamation "the day of Easter - the day of joy."

It is surely not anything new to note that everything Karl Barth wrote or the manner in which he expressed himself had been carefully thought through and clearly focussed. It is true that now and then, when reading his

works, the structure of his statements appears com-
plicated. But upon closer inspection and repeated reading
it becomes clear that he could not proceed in any other
way in saying what he wanted to say, illuminating it from
all sides and making it credible in every context. How
often one finds passages which stand there like a solid
structure that cannot be shaken. Here is such an example.
In one of his letters he wrote how he thought about eternal
life "according to the guidance of the Revelation of John,
as well as that of the entire Holy Scriptures."

> Eternal life is not another and second life, beyond
> the present one. It is this life, but the reverse side
> which God sees although it is as yet hidden from us
> - this life in relation to what He has done for the
> whole world, and therefore for us too, in Jesus
> Christ. We thus wait and hope, even in view of our
> death, for our manifestation with Him, with Jesus
> Christ who was raised again from the dead, in the
> glory of not only the judgment but also the grace
> of God. The new thing will be that the cover of
> tears, death, suffering, crying, and pain that now
> lies over our present life will be lifted, that the
> decree of God fulfilled in Jesus Christ will stand
> before our eyes, and that it will be the subject not
> only of our deepest shame but also of our joyful
> thanks and praise.[3]

Karl Barth once surmised that Wolfgang Amadeus

Mozart may well have *heard* in his great freedom what he then was allowed to play in the same great freedom, according to the measure given to him.[4] Is it presumptuous to apply at times a like surmise to Karl Barth's "hearing" and the transmission of what he heard?

Karl Barth had the rare gift of not only living his life in an intensive fashion but also of observing it - as if from a higher plane. This characteristic cannot be specifically explained. It was unmistakably present. He did not dispute this fact in my presence. I suspect that his refreshing laughter about himself cannot be understood apart from this gift nor the sharp criticism he applied to himself and his work. From such a perspective one may perhaps also understand the courage with which he faced times of illness, a courage that permitted him never to lose his inner equilibrium. Every time there was even a slight improvement, marked every time by the fact that he picked up his pipe again, the first thing which returned was the joy in his work.

But his heart grew continuously weaker, affected by several operations. He spent the second to last day of his life, Sunday, December 8, 1968, with my mother-in-law in our home. In the afternoon he and I visited, as we did every Sunday, Lollo v. Kirschbaum, who had been con-

---

3. *Karl Barth, Letters 1961-1968*, ed. Jürgen Fangmeier and Hinrich Stovesandt, transl. Geoffrey Bromiley; Grand Rapids, Michigan: Wm. B. Eerdmans Publishing Company, 1981, p. 9.
4. cf. *Wolfgang Amadeus Mozart*, 10.ed.; Zurich: TVZ Verlag, 1978, p. 45-6.

fined by a brain disease for three years to the Sonnenhalde clinic at Riehen. As always we sang at her bedside "Now Thank We All Our God." As we were driving my father-in-law quite suddenly talked of his own impending death. He would really like to be buried in such a way that his grave, like that of Mozart, could not be found. But out of consideration for his family he would give up that wish. He strongly requested that a simple grave would be chosen and the headstone not be elaborate. We spoke of much more before we drove up to our house in order to pick up my mother-in-law and drive over to the Bruderholz. To my astonishment Papa did not remain in the car. He asked to be helped out of his seat and said, "You won't be rid of me that quickly today." After spending considerable time with us, that same evening at the Bruderholz he presented our son Dieter an edition of the *Church Dogmatics* and gave mother-in-law her Christmas present. On Monday next he was wholly absorbed in preparing an address, interrupted only late that night by two telephone calls from people whom, in characteristic fashion, only *he* could help with some encouraging words. During the night of December 10 he closed his eyes forever.

The years do not help to overcome the sorrow over the loss of my beloved father-in-law. The knowledge of his peaceful death is for me both a light and a guidepost. "Remember your teachers, those who first spoke God's word to you; and reflecting upon the outcome of their life and work, follow the example of their faith." (Hebrews 13: 7; N.E.B.)